Published by Mobius Publishing Limited

Delsey Luggage Aero Frame 29 Inch Spinner

"Great line of luggage, we travel nonstop and they have heald up great!"

"Great Quality, Size and Value ...Perfect Checked Bag!"

- Made from durable material for long lasting use
- Four double-spinner wheels assure smooth mobility
- 12.25x21.75x32 inches

Aero frame combines style, quality and convenience in a bag that features four double spinner wheels for superior maneuverability, and a unique aluminum frame locking system for maximum security.

To Get It Now, Visit tiny.cc/mpub/travel

Bonus: FREE   E-Book!

As a special thank you to my readers, I am giving away free copies of *Backyard Chickens: The Ultimate Guide*. Enjoy eggs from your backyard while they're still warm! Reconnect with nature and your food by having your own chickens. It's easier than you think.

To get instant access to this book and more awesome resources, visit the link below:

Tiny.cc/mpub/free-gift-backyard-chickens

As an added bonus, subscribers will be given a chance to get exclusive sneak peaks of upcoming books and a chance to get free copies with no strings attached. Don't worry, we treat your e-mail with the respect it deserves. You won't get any spammy emails!!!

Contents

Part 1

Introduction

Oh Iceland, one of those countries that makes you shake your head in confusion when you think about it, and not for a bad reason, it's just that its landscape is, well, strange.

But what does this mean?

Iceland it's a rather small (It's about the size of Ohio) country placed at the topmost part of the globe, it is a vast volcanic territory in constant shaping from many natural forces such as geysers, (ice-covered) volcanoes, rumbles, glaciers and boiling mud pools!

As such, we see some very strange combination of natural elements, such as icy volcanoes, geysers and glaciers, indeed a strange sight.

After all, can you believe that in a territory as small as 40,000 sq miles has something like:

While also having something like:

Truly astounding isn't it?

Iceland is a beautiful island, so I congratulate you for choosing this marvelous piece of the earth as your travel destination!

In this handy guide, I'll walk you through a few elemental topics to enjoy your trip to Iceland at its fullest!

I'll tell you about:

- **What to bring**: There are a few tips you'll need for packing clothes!

- **The Icelandic Experience**: Everything you need to know before your trip.

- **Things to do**: There are activities and places you **absolutely** need to check in your trip.

- **Interesting facts**: Everyone loves interesting facts, and knowing these can help you a lot at engaging conversation with the locals!

Part 2

Preparation

If you plan on going to sunny areas or beaches, pack your usual bathing suit and towel (don't forget to bring sunscreen), depending on the season you travel and the activities you plan to do, bring appropriate shoes and clothes, in case you want to perform specific outdoor activities you'll likely be able to rent any equipment you need in Iceland.

Bring all your recording stuff! Your camera, chargers, spare films and SD cards, if you like writing bring an ample journal and a few pens.

Just to be sure, bring physical maps if you plan on hiking a lot.

Risking overstating the obvious, please, bring warm clothes! Iceland can get, well, icy, and if you're like me (I can't handle cold for the life of me) then do yourself a favor and bring lots of warm clothes.

Be sure to leave space for any souvenirs you desire to bring back to your friends and family! After all, what kind of person would you be if you went to such a beautiful reach and didn't bring something back for your family or friends?

There are plenty options for staying in Iceland, so be sure to talk with your travel agent or arrange it yourself, you can find the perfect spot right now, so be sure to make the bookings before actually arriving the island.

Don't worry, practically all the places you can stay in Iceland will have Internet, but don't lock yourself to your phone/laptop when you're there!

Oh, one last thing, there's not many fast-food brands in Iceland (no McDonald's, nor Starbucks for that matter) so you'll have to make do with the local cuisine, but hey, that's even better! You're already accustomed to the food in your native place, so open your mind (and your mouth) to the fine delicacies of Iceland during your stay!

Part 3

The Icelandic Experience

Given the marvelous natural conditions of Iceland, what may be day-to-day stuff becomes a whole new experience in Iceland.

With geothermal lagoons, glaciers, the Aurora Borealis and icy volcanoes, anything from a simple stroll can turn into an almost cinematic experience.

But Iceland is much more than just its tremendous landscape, it is packed with Icelanders, whose culture is rich and ample, their arts include from the traditional crafts of weaving, wood carving, knitting and silver-smithing to music, literature and painting.

Icelandic culture is simply fantastical, you can find live musical plays as well as visual arts and handicrafts everywhere.

Before sailing to Iceland, let me give you a quick rundown of things you'll need to know before going to the island.

- **Currency**: (ISK) Icelandic króna (krónur in plural) you will find banknotes from 500 to 5000 krónur, although, credit cards are way better, and don't worry even in the farthest reaches of the land you can still make use of them, but you've got ATMs available in all towns.

- **Language**:I bet this one had you worried the most at first, but don't worry! The official language of Iceland is the Icelandic since 2011, and several actions have been performed on order to keep the language active, but English is widely-spoken in the Island, so don't let that scare you!

- **Phone**: There's plenty coverage for

mobile phones, and visitors with GSM phones can make roaming calls, but if you plan staying a while, purchasing a local SIM card might be worth it!

- **Time Zone**: Iceland uses the Western European Time Zone (GMT/UTC+0:00)

Part 4

Seasons To Go

Depending on what you want (and your budget) you might decide to go in the High, Mid or Low seasons.

- High-Season: Between Jun-Aug, the tourist count descends, which means that prices peak, so preemptive bookings are a great idea, during this season you got endless daylight and a lot of festivals and activities to assist. All roads are open which means you can get a lot of hiking going in this season.

- Mid-Season: Between May-Sept, breezy weather and occasional snows in-land, this season is great if you'd like smaller crowds and lower prices.

- Low-Season: Between Oct-Apr, a handful of minor roads are shut due to the harsher weather, but say hello to all winter activities like skiing, snowshoeing and ice cave exploration, brief days and longer nights with some Northern Lights sightings!

Part 5

Icelandic Geography

Being more closer to continental Europe than North America, the island is usually regarded as part of Europe.

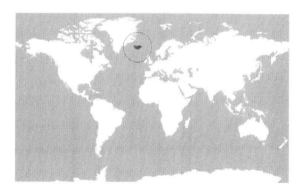

This is because historical, political, practical and even cultural reasons, geologically, the Island has parts of both continental plates included.

Globally, Iceland is considered the 18th largest island, while (after Great Britain) being considered the 2nd largest in Europe.

About 30 small islands are part of Iceland's jurisdiction, like the Vestmannaeyjar archipelago.

Two thirds of Iceland is a tundra, while only 23% percent of the land is vegetated.

Part 6

Icelandic Climate

Iceland's coast climate is sub-arctic, but the warm North Atlantic Current generates higher annual temperatures in comparison to similar places with the same latitude.

Contrary to popular belief, Iceland's coast is pretty much ice-free through winter, and generally speaking, the south coast is much warmer and wetter than the north.

Part 7

Things To Do In In Iceland

All these are the author's opinion, but nonetheless, if you're interested by all means do some of these (or all of them, they're great!).

Sighting the Northern Lights

Basically mandatory, you can't just go to Iceland and not gaze upon the beautiful colored sky.

If you're interested in **why** does this happen, well basically, solar flares are drawn to our planet's magnetic field towards the north pole, and it results in these ethereal veils of colored light silently dancing in the sky, however, if you want to gaze upon this beautiful natural phenom, you'll have to be anytime between October and April.

The Fimmvörðuháls Trek

If you're interested in treks, and you're willing to spend a day-long 23k long trek then Fimmvörðuháls will give you just that, beginning at Skógafoss' cascades, hike up to the hinterland and stroll through the beautiful parade of waterfalls and lay your eyes on what remains of the Eyjafjallajökull eruption, and end your trek in Þórsmörk.

Truly a great experience to be had if you have the wanderer's thirst!

Visiting the Tröllaskagi

Peninsula

The Peninsula of Tröllaskagi is sited with the beautiful towns of Siglufjörður and Ólafsfjörðu, the peninsula's scenery is magnificent and strolling through the cinematic panoramas and quality hiking spots will surely become yet another precious activity you partake in Iceland.

You can even take ferries to the offshore islands of Grímsey and Hrísey!

Visiting Iceland's Capital: Reykjavík

By international standards, Iceland's capital is rather small, but there are all sorts of things you can do in the capital!

You can check the excellent museums that preserve so much of the medieval era, shop all sorts of local objects and attires, or simply relax in one of the city's coffeehouses (the amount of coffeehouses in the city is truly staggering) and taste the local flavors of designer coffees and microbrews.

Visiting the Blue Lagoon

Another mandatory site you must visit during your stay at Iceland!

I could give you a long rundown of why you should visit the magical healing natural spa that is the Blue Lagoon, but simply put, do you really need more justification to visit it? It's a cultural staple of Iceland, and you're bound to have a great time in this geothermic haven and the plus side is that this is an activity equally performed by the locals!

Visit Þingvellir

Declared as an UNESCO World Heritage Site, in this beautiful national park sits the national shrine of Iceland, and it holds one of the oldest pieces of Icelandic history, and for that matter, of the history of the world, as the oldest existing parliament in the world assembled there in 930 AD.

While being historically relevant is fascinating enough, its natural beauty just gives you more reasons to go there!

Visit Snæfellsjökull, First National Park of Iceland

It reaches from the seashore to a mountaintop, and it houses one of the most famous glaciers of the earth!

This glacier is said to be one of the "seven great energy entrances of the earth" and it served as a setting for the critically acclaimed novel *Journey to the Center of the Earth*

Go Horseback Riding

Iceland is home to one of a unique breed of horses, and they won't be found anywhere else, if that isn't convincing enough, you'll do well to remember that Iceland is also known for its quality equine history! So mount a horse and gallop across the landscapes!

Go Caving

Caving is an extreme exploration trip! Getting yourself in one of the many tours to explore the caves, lava tubes and craters around the land is certainly a memory you will never forget, and this kind of activity is one of a kind, so do your inner explorer a favor and sign for this!

Check the Viking World Museum!

There's no better way of truly living the Nordic experience without Vikings, and fortunately for you, there's a whole museum dedicated to Vikings in Iceland!

Enjoy the five exhibition museums dedicated to Vikings, and bask in their history and culture (you can take glimpses at the fabled Viking longboats!)

Bask In the Natural Beauty of Landmannalaugar

Landmannalaugar is one of those places that crown Iceland champion in exotic landscapes!

Just look at that! The mountains are beautiful

and the colors are alive and vibrant; the valleys and plains are all coated in lush grass and flowers, the sight alone is pristine and rejuvenating.

Another great activity you can do in Landmannalaugar is taking a dip in the hot rivers, in fact, the rough translation of Landmannalaugar is *"People's Pool"* so by all means enjoy the finest (and free) thermal waters that the Icelandic Highlands can offer, just remember to pack adequate supplies because the road is hard and there's not much you can find there to supply!

Adventure Into the Skaftafell Ice Cave

Within the national park of Vatnajökull, lies the impressive ice cave of Skaftafell!

During wintertime, glacial rivers retract and freeze, forming these natural ice caves, and many ice caves are formed in different locations each year in this fashion!

You won't find a better adrenaline-filled adventure anywhere else, so if you're feeling daring then prepare yourself for the ice caves of Vatnajökull!

It is of utmost importance that you go to these caves with a certified guide, as there are many factors that play a role in the safety of the trip, and the aid of an expert on the matter will not only make the trip better (and also insightful) but it will make it safe.

Most groups for cave-exploring are about 12 persons, and you definitely need to bring your own supplies, especially warm clothing, layers upon layers of warm clothing if you're like me.

Give the Hallgrímskirkja Church a Visit

Regarded as both the largest church as well as the tallest structure of Iceland, Hallgrímskirkja is a Lutheran church in Reykjavík.

Impressive and imposing, this architectural feat is named after Hallgrímur Pétursson, an Icelandic clergyman and poet from the 17th century.

Designed in 1937 by a Guðjón Samuel thanks to his inspiration from shapes and forms born out of basalt rocks, Hallgrímskirkja began its construction in 1945, and 40 years later, in 1986, the church was done.

Outside of the church lies a statue of Leif Eriksson, a fabled explorer from the 10th century, it was a gift from the United States, as a way of honoring Iceland's parliament 1000th anniversary in 1930.

Yes! Iceland's parliament has over 1000 years, it was founded in 930 AD.

Embrace the Natural Beauty of the Gullfoss Waterfall

In the Hvítá river you will find the Gullfoss waterfall, renowned for being amongst the most popular attractions for tourists in Iceland and the reasons are quite obvious.

The vibrant colors of Iceland's landscape coupled with the majestic waterfall team up to deliver an almost cinematic experience of nature, the very edge of the fall is obscured from view, and it almost feels like the river vanishes into thin air.

It looks even more impressive during winter!

Part 8

Bonus Trip: Game of Thrones Filming Locations

This full-day guided tour starts in Reykjavik, and it aims to take you into a marvelous 6-hour tour to cover several filming locations used in the hit television series "Game of Thrones."

Reserve a tour, and a pickup will take you from several selected hotels—alternatively, you can make your own way to a meeting point. From there, you will hop into a climate-controlled coach, and set onwards across Iceland's fantastic scenery; your guide will give an introduction to the role of Iceland during the filming of the show.

One of the first stops is Thingvellir National Park, you can disembark to check out its gorge, which features the European and American tectonic plates, slowly drifting apart.

After that, the trip stops in Lake Thingvallavatn—This is not a filming location, but it is simply wonderful!

Shortly after, check the waterfall Thórufoss where one of Daenery's dragons attacked a goat. Catch some of the Icelandic four-legged stars of the show: Westeros horses. Pass along the Almannagjá gorge used to depict the Bloody Gate of Eyrie. And finally, the Thjorsárdalur valley where a peaceful farming village was struck by Wildlings and the Thenns.

There's a lot to see on this tour, and it operates all day, so don't miss your chance!

Part 9

Interesting Facts About Iceland

Iceland is already an interesting parade, but I'll give you some great tips you probably didn't know about Iceland.

Part 10

Internet Usage In Iceland

While Iceland has a really tiny population by international standards (as such, comparing the number of internet users vs a big country would be meaningless) it is the country with the biggest percentage of population utilizing internet, ranked at a whopping 98.20% of the total population!

Part 11

Literacy In Iceland

Iceland is known for being culture-rich country, so it doesn't surprise that its literacy rate is amongst the highest in the world!

A usual Christmas gift in Iceland is a book in fact!

Part 12

Elves In Iceland

Also known as the *"hidden folk"* or *"Huldufólk"* in Icelandic, they're the "elves" of Iceland they're usually depicted with elvish/gnomish looks, dressed in 19th century Icelandic clothing and, above all, with the natural ability of remaining invisible.

In fact, folk beliefs hold that one shouldn't throw rocks because of the possibility of hitting one of the hidden folk.

Part 13

Iceland Is Home To Lazy Town

The Icelander author of Lazy Town goes by the name of Magnús Scheving, and the studios are located in Garðabær.

Part 14

Iceland Has No Army

Iceland is the only country of the NATO (North Atlantic Treaty Organization) that doesn't have a standing army, they have however a good national police, as well as non-police military forces such as their skilled Coastal Guard, they have an agreement with the United States for defense.

Part 15

Comedian Mayor

Born 2 of January 1967, Icelandic actor and comedian, Jón Gnarr served as the mayor of Reykjavík from 2010 to 2014.

He formed a political party as a satire, but it shortly became a success when he won the elections.

He made many joke promises through his campaign as well as his period as mayor, and one of the promises of his campaign was that he wasn't going to fulfill any of the promises.

Part 16
Cold Naps

Icelandic babies are left outside to nap in freezing temperatures. It is not uncommon to see a pram outside a coffee shop, parents grabbing a cup while the baby sleeps. Or to see one outside a house, because many babies in Iceland nap outside once a day or more, regardless what season it is.

Babies napping outside in the cold in their prams aren't an uncommon sight in Iceland, in fact, they're pretty common, and if you walk around you will definitely find babies napping in their prams outside Icelandic homes or coffee shops.

The purpose of this nap is to help babies adapt better to the cold (essential for an Icelander) as well as helping his well-being overall as the cold, clean air does wonders to one's respiratory system.

Part 17

Naming Laws

There are several strict laws regarding what names are (or not) allowed in Iceland, in order to preserve Icelandic language and culture.

Names that were not previously accepted need to undergo deliberation before the Icelandic Naming Committee, which either accepts the name (if it abides by their laws regarding Icelandic names) or rejects them, and in that case the parents are forced to find another name for their child.

Kristján Jóhann Björn Helgi
Jón Einar Gunnar
Ragnar Arnar Sigurður Bjarni
Magnús Halldór
Stefán Árni Guðmundur Kristinn
Pétur
Gísli Ólafur

52

Part 18

Everlasting Light

During summertime, you will find that it hardly gets dark at all. This is because of Iceland's location.

Day and night merge into one, and it seems like the day actually never ends. During these days, Icelanders don't sleep as much, and in turn, many "midnight" activities arise, including midnight golf tournaments!

Part 19

No Surnames

Surnames (in the traditional sense) are non-existent for Icelanders. Icelandic surnames are just a cue to point that you're the son/daughter of your father/mother.

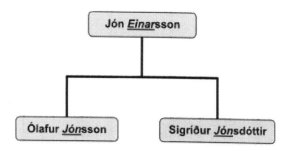

Regardless of formalities, first names are almost always used for addressing someone, and even their phone books list their subscribers with their names, rather than surnames.

Part 20

Conclusion

I hope you found this guide useful, and sincerely hope you enjoy your trip to Iceland, it is truly a beautiful parade and without a doubt it will become a trip like none other!

Iceland is a magnificent country blessed with one of the most impressive landscape varieties in the world! So be sure to enjoy the true beauty of the country by hiking, visiting waterfalls and enjoying the beaches.

But don't forget the rich cultural-historical heritage that Iceland has, so by all means assist to the plenty festivals held at the land, visit the many museums that dot the capital (especially the Viking ones) and enjoy your time hearing the locals and their folklore!

We can now bid this guide as "completed", I thank you for taking the time to read through it, and once again, I hope you enjoy your trip, goodbye!

Sign up for Mobius Publishing updates and receive a **FREE BOOK** immediately! Visit tiny.cc/mpub to sign up.

You can also get information on upcoming

book launches, free book promotions and much more!

Visit tiny.cc/mpub/rhodes where you can check out all my other books.

You can also reach me on Twitter at @MobiusBooks or on Facebook at @Mobius.Publishing.

Thank you and good luck,

Antony

EBags Professional

Slim Laptop Backpack

"Simply a great bag. Designed and built well. A pocket for everything, and great for organization."

"My favorite go-to bag"

- Limited Lifetime Warranty against defects in materials and workmanship

- Uber organized with fully padded lockable laptop and tablet compartments, crush-proof AC adaptor garage and zippered water bottle pocket

- Fits laptops 1.5 D x 12.25" W x 16.5" to 17.5" H if pad removed and tablet compartment is 8.125 W x 11.5 H

- Easily converts from backpack to briefcase and includes vertical and horizontal luggage handle pass-thru panels

You deserve a bag you can't live without. Isolated rapid-access compartments protect your laptop, iPad or tablet, sequester your printed materials, force you to be neat organized by eliminating clutter zones, in a package that defies its published cubic inch capacity. It's like turbo charging a compact car. Buckle up it's going to be a great ride

To Get It Now, Visit tiny.cc/mpub/travel

More from Mobius Publishing

DON'T FORGET! Get your bonus book: Backyard Chickens: The Ultimate Guide

As a special thank you to my readers, I am giving away free copies of *Backyard Chickens: The Ultimate Guide*. Enjoy eggs from your backyard while they're still warm! Reconnect with nature and your food by having your own chickens. It's easier than you think.

To get instant access to this book and more awesome resources, visit the link below:

Tiny.cc/mpub/free-gift-backyard-chickens

As an added bonus, subscribers will be given a chance to get exclusive sneak peaks of upcoming books and a chance to get free copies with no strings attached. Don't worry, we treat your e-mail with the respect it deserves. You won't get any spammy emails!!!

You might also be interested in...

Taste of Scandinavia: 40 Handpicked, Delicious and Healthy Nordic Recipes

"Wonderfully presented cookbook and guide to real Scandinavian cuisine"—Val

"Cause to celebrate a little known cuisine ... a delightful culinary experience."—Simon

"... a book with loads of possibilities! Found some of my new favorite recipes"—Evelyn

Looking For
Something New?

Embark On a Culinary Adventure To Scandinavia

Best-selling author Antony Rhodes teams up with award-winning chef Hanna Gustavsson to bring you **40 classic recipes** from her motherland.

Experience a **grand tour of Scandinavian cuisine**. With the multitude of flavors, there's something everyone will love. These exceptional dishes known to the northerners in Iceland, Norway, Finland and Sweden will **liven up your dinner table** and keep you coming back for more.

Learn How To Make These Awesome Nordic Recipes:

Main Dishes

- Smoked Trout Creme Fraiche
- Asparagus and Smoked Salmon Tart
- Swedish Beef Burgers (Biff à La

Lindström)

- Potato Gratin With Juniper
- Crayfish With Dill (Kräftor Med Dill)
- Skinkstek
- Spaetzle
- Scandinavian Meatballs
- Stuffed Cabbage Rolls

Appetizers

- Scandinavian Ceviche
- Scandinavian Gravlax
- Scandinavian Shrimp Canapés
- Scandinavian Crab Cakes

Breakfast Dishes

- Potato Rösti and Fried Eggs
- Einkorn Bread
- Iceland Shrimp Salad
- Rye Bread With Apple (Rågbröd Med äpple)
- Swedish Oven Pancake With Bacon

Lunch and Snacks

- Frugtsalat (Danish Fruit Salad)

- Mushroom Tart
- Mushroom Risotto

Soups and Stews

- Sailor's Beef Stew (Sjömansbiff)
- Fiskesuppe (Norwegian Cod and Root Vegetable Chowder)
- Wild Mushroom Soup (Svampsoppa)
- Cod Stew
- Seafood Stew (Cacciucco)
- Pumpkin Soup
- Rotfruktsgryta - Swedish Root Vegetable Stew
- Cream of Carrot Soup
- Kalops (Beef Stew)
- Creamy Norwegian Fish Soup

Desserts and Beverages

- Apple Pudding
- Almond Cakes
- Rhubarb Cordial
- Chocolate Balls (Chokladbollar)
- Saffron Cake (Saffranspannkaka)

Free Bonus E-book: *Backyard Chickens: the Ultimate Guide*

And much, much more!

Don't Miss Out On These Unique Recipes and Get Your Copy Today!

Go to tiny.cc/mpub and search for *scandinavian cookbook* to see the entire book.

Preview of First Chapter:

Part 1

Main Dishes

Smoked Trout Creme Fraiche

Make a traditional smørrebrød.

Serves: 4

Total time: ~30 minutes

Cook time: 2-3 minutes or as long as it takes toast bread slices

Ingredients

1. thinly sliced red onions - 1/4 cup

2. sugar – 1 tbsp

3. red wine vinegar – 1/4 cup

4. kosher salt – 1/2 tsp

5. hot water – 1/4 cup

6. lemon zest - 1 tsp

7. pumpernickel bread - 12 slices

8. freshly ground black pepper - 1/4 tsp

9. crème fraîche - 1/2 cup

10. Smoked trout - 12 Oz

11. Dill

Method

1. Add vinegar, sugar onions and salt to a bowl with ¼ cup hot water and allow to pickle for 30 minutes

2. Preheat a grill and toast bread slices

3. Combine crème fraîche with lemon zest and freshly ground black pepper in a bowl

4. Lay out toasted bread and spoon the mixture on top.

5. Place 1 ounce of smoked trout on top with a few slices of pickled onions and garnish with dill

To see the rest of *Taste of*

Scandinavia: 40 Handpicked, Delicious and Healthy Nordic Recipes by Hanna Gustavsson and Antony Rhodes, search on Amazon or visit tiny.cc/mpub and search for *scandinavian cookbook*

Also consider:

The Dutch Oven Cookbook: 25 Handpicked, Delicious & Healthy Recipes For Every Day

"Best of all, my family ACTUALLY ATE them, and rated each dish a 'make this one again, please'."—Alfonzo

"My New Best Friend for Fuss-Free One-Pot Meals"—Tara

"Minimal prep time, recipes taste great!"—Lori

Your Dutch

Must-Have Oven

Cookbook For Your Dutch Oven!

Are You Looking For Delicious Easy To Make Dutch Oven Recipes That Save You Time and Money? This Book Could Be the Answer You're Looking For...

We all know that eating healthy is hard and cooking healthy food every day is even harder! Dutch ovens have taken off in popularity because they solve both issues at once. By making large healthy meals in one setting, you can have **nutritious and delicious meals that will last** for days. No more need to waste time cooking and cleaning every day!

This book is designed to empower you by providing **essential Dutch Oven cooking techniques** along with tasty recipes to help you make delicious, nutritious meals.

You Get:

- How to choose your Dutch Oven
- How to care for your Dutch Oven
- How to clean Your Dutch Oven
- Other Useful Tips
- 25 Recipes For EVERY Meal - Breakfast, Lunch, Dinner and Dessert!

Learn How To Make These Awesome Recipes:

Breads

- Banana Bread
- Buttermilk Cornbread
- Monkey Bread
- Ginger Bread
- Mexican Corn Bread

Main Dishes

- Brown Sugar and Maple Steak Bites

- Vegetarian Chili
- Malatang
- Jambalaya
- Chicken Cordon Bleu Casserole
- Deep Dish Pizza
- Ratatouille
- German Sauerbraten
- Cheese Steak Soup
- Hawaiian meatballs

Vegetables

- Green Bean Casserole
- Vegetable Noodle Casserole
- Vegetable Parmesan
- Hot Pot Potatoes
- Zucchini Casserole

Desserts

- Orange Glaze Cake
- Skor Cake
- Peach Cobbler
- Raspberry Cobbler
- Chocolate Turtle Cake

And much, much more!

Don't Miss Out On These Delicious Recipes and Get Your Copy Today!

Go to tiny.cc/mpub and search for *dutch oven* to see the entire book.

Preview of First Chapter:

Part 1

Dutch Oven Care, Tips and Tricks

Choose Your Dutch Oven

The Dutch oven is well suited to almost any type of scenario, and as such, it has been adapted to suit all types of situations. If you plan to use it on camping trips with large groups, then you will be better off with a pot that's fourteen to sixteen inches in diameter. At ten to twelve inches, a family would find greater utility. Smaller sizes, as small as eight inches could also be found.

You may find Dutch ovens with bail handles made of heavy gauge wire to be exceedingly useful in almost any situation, especially if the bail handle is securely attached via tangs on the sides of the pot. Riveted tangs are to be avoided. If you are partial to a lighter pot that's easier to carry, then you may appreciate the aluminum varieties that can be found. Aluminum Dutch ovens do not require seasoning to ensure durability over time. Be advised however, that aluminum takes longer to heat and does not retain heat as long as the traditional cast iron versions. Cast iron varieties require care to provide long service to the Dutch oven purist. To keep the surfaces usable and intact, these pots must be seasoned and oiled. Users find that the longer heat retention and shorter heat-up time, render the time tested cast iron Dutch oven, a monolith in their cookware arsenal.

Care For Your Dutch Oven

Season your cast iron Dutch oven before use to ensure that it does not rust and that flavors from the foods you prepare are not absorbed into the porous cast iron. A Dutch oven that is properly seasoned will not require much cleaning and will get better with age.

Your cast iron adventure begins with the following steps:

1. Heat cookware and peel off label. If there are any irregularities in the underside of the metal such as burns or tarnishes - file them away.

2. Wash, rinse and dry with warm, soapy water.

3. Oil cookware. Spread an even film of oil over the entire surface of the pot. One tablespoon of oil should do.

4. Add more oil and heat. Add enough oil to cover the bottom of the utensil. Place in medium oven until oil is hot and thin (but not smoking!).

5. Lift Dutch oven off of heat and rotate so that oil re-coats the entire surface.

6. Add oil and heat at 200-250 for one hour. Leave utensil in oven over-night.

7. Wipe with a paper towel before use.

Clean Your Dutch Oven

Never use soap on cast iron cookware. Bring water to a boil and gently scrub with a sponge to remove stuck on food. Rinse and allow to air dry, then heat until the pot is warm to the touch. Apply a thin coat of oil to the inside of the oven and to the underside of the lid.

Other Useful Tips

Have on hand a good pair of gloves to assist with the handling of the Dutch oven. Leather gloves work well for this purpose and a pair of hot pot pliers can extend your capabilities in lifting the lid or grasping the handle in high heat situations. You may also want to keep a shovel handy if you plan to heat with coals.

A Quick Guide To Cooking

Techniques With the Dutch Oven

We're almost about to dive into the recipe section, just keep the following techniques in mind before you embark on your adventures with the Dutch oven.

To Roast

Place coals on the lid of the oven and beneath to oven at a 1 to 1 ratio. 20 coals should give about 500 degrees.

To Bake

Place more coals on top of the lid than underneath the oven at a ratio of 1 to 3 so that more heat comes from the top.

To Fry or Boil

All heat should come from beneath the pot.

To Stew or Simmer

Place almost all the coals beneath the pot at a ratio of 1 to 4

Now you're primed and ready to begin cooking!

To see the rest of *The Dutch Oven Cookbook: 25 Handpicked, Delicious & Healthy Recipes For Every Day* by Antony Rhodes, search on Amazon or visit tiny.cc/mpub and search for *dutch oven*

Made in the USA
Middletown, DE
19 November 2018